COGAT®
TEST PREP GRADE 1

- **Grade 1 Level 7 Form 7**
- **One Full-Length Practice Test**
- **136 Practice Questions**
- **Answer Key**
- **Sample Questions for Each Test Area**
- **54 Additional Bonus Questions Online**

Nicole Howard

PLEASE LEAVE US A REVIEW!

Thank you for selecting this book.

We'd love to get your feedback on the website where you purchased this book.

By leaving a review, you give us the opportunity to improve our work.

Nicole Howard and the SkilledChildren.com Team

www.skilledchildren.com

TABLE OF CONTENTS

INTRODUCTION

The Cognitive Abilities Test (CogAT®) is an assessment of a student's verbal, quantitative, and nonverbal reasoning ability. Administered to grades K-12, the CogAT® is designed to identify gifted students.

This book will increase the student's chances of success by providing an overview of the different types of questions for Grade 1, Level 7, Form 7 of the CogAT® test.

A comprehensive practice test and its answer key, with clear explanations, are all included in this book to allow students to understand the testing structure and the different types of questions within it.

Additionally, by reading this book, you will gain free online access to 54 bonus practice questions. You will find the link and password on the last page of this book.

It is highly recommended to read this introductory section to understand how the CogAT® works.

An Overview of the CogAT® Level 7

The CogAT® is administered to a group of children at a single time.

There are three autonomous sections of the test, specifically:

1. Verbal testing

2. Nonverbal testing

3. Quantitative testing

These autonomous sections can be used individually, and some children may only be asked to take one or two parts of the test based on the evaluations of their tutors.

Each sub-test can be difficult for everyone who has never seen the test previously. Additionally, without proper training, it is not possible to acquire the skills that will allow children to solve the questions.

The Length and the Complete Format of the Test

The total time given for the three sections of the Level 7 test is 112 minutes.

Tests will vary, depending on the grades that are being assessed, but the Level 7 is divided into 136 multiple-choice questions. The questions are categorized as follows:

Verbal Section

- "Sentence completion" has 16 questions.

- "Picture classification" has 16 questions.

- "Picture analogies" has 16 questions.

Nonverbal Section

- "Figure matrices" has 16 questions.

- "Paper folding skills" has 12 questions.

- "Figure classifications" has 16 questions.

Quantitative Section

- "Understanding number analogies" has 16 questions.

- "The number series" has 16 questions.

- "Solving number puzzles" has 12 questions.

The total number of questions for these three sections equals 136.

The Test Breakdown

The verbal section of the test assesses the child's use of language, particularly the skill in identifying the correlation between words. These questions often involve the use of analogy.

The verbal section of the Level 7 of CogAT® has three subtypes of questions that need to be answered:

1. Sentence Completion: The teacher reads aloud a question. Children must choose the picture that best answers the question in a complete, logical way.

2. Picture Classification: Students are required to classify pictures into like groups in this section. They will be given three pictures that have something in common and will be asked to identify a fourth picture that completes the set.

3. Picture Analogies: Students are required to identify analogies. They will be given two pictures that go together, as well as a third, unrelated picture. They must pick the most fitting pair for the third picture from the answer choices given, based on the logic used for the original pair of pictures.

The nonverbal section of the test is designed to assess a student's ability to reason and think beyond what they've already been taught. This section includes geometric shapes and figures that aren't normally seen in the classroom. This will force children to use different methods to solve problems. There are also three subtypes of questions that need to be answered in the nonverbal section of the CogAT®:

1. Figure Classification: Students are required to analyze three similar figures and apply the next appropriate figure to complete the sequence.

2. Figure Matrices: Children are introduced to basic matrices (2x2 grids) to solve for the missing shapes within them. Three of the four squares in the matrices will already be filled out, and they must choose which image fills the last square from the options provided.

3. Paper Folding Skills: Children are introduced to paper folding and will need to ascertain where punched holes in a folded piece of paper would be after the paper is unfolded.

The quantitative section introduces abstract reasoning and problem-solving skills to learners and is one of the most challenging sections in the test. This section is also structured into three different parts:

1. Interpreting a Series of Numbers: Children are required to determine which string of beads is needed to complete a sequence that follows a specific pattern, by observing an abacus.

2. Solving Number Puzzles: Children see two trains. They must choose the answer picture that makes the second train carrying an equal number of things as the first one.

3. Understanding Number Analogies: Children will be provided with 2x2 basic matrices. Each box of the matrices contains a certain number of objects. In the lower row, the child must identify the same relationship as in the upper row and select the answer option that best fits the box with the question mark.

How to Use the Content in This Book

Since the CogAT® is an important test in all students' schooling careers, the correct amount of preparation must be performed. Children that take the time to adequately prepare will inevitably do better than students that don't.

This book will help you prepare your children before test day and will expose them to the format of the test so they'll know what to expect. This book includes:

- One full-length CogAT® Level 7 practice questionnaire.

- Question examples for teachers/parents to help children approach all of the questions on the test with confidence and determination.

- Answer key with clear explanations.

Take the time to adequately go through all of the sections to fully understand how to teach this information to younger students. Many of the abstract versions of these questions will be difficult for some children to understand, so including some visual aids during preparation times will be greatly beneficial.

Tips and Strategies for Test Preparation

The most important factor regarding the CogAT® is to apply the time and effort to the learning process for the test and make the preparation periods as stress-free as possible. Although everyone will experience stress in today's world, being able to cope with that stress will be a useful tool. All children will experience varying amounts of anxiety before these types of tests, but one of the ways to adequately combat this is by taking the time to prepare for them.

The CogAT® has difficult questions from the very beginning. Some of the questions will range from difficult to very abstract, regardless of the age group or level.

It's necessary to encourage children to use different types of strategies to answer questions that they find challenging.

Children will get questions incorrect in some of the sections; it's vital to help them understand what errors they made, so they can learn from their mistakes.

PRACTICE TEST VERBAL BATTERY

This section of the CogAT® test assesses the child's use of language, particularly the skill in identifying the correlation between words. These questions often involve the use of analogy.

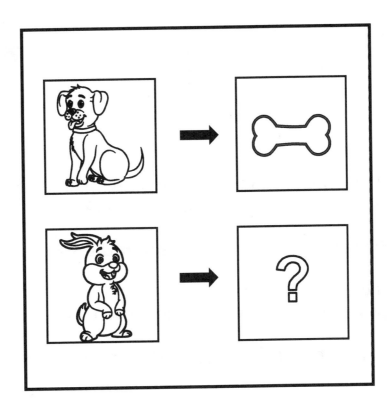

Picture Analogies

A picture analogy traces a similarity between a pair of objects and another pair of objects.

Example

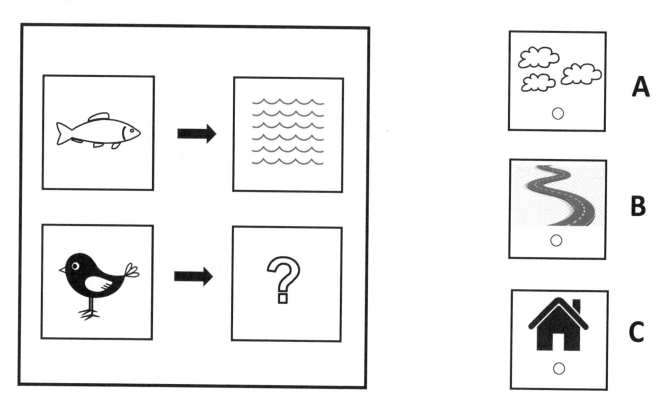

- First, identify the relationship between the first pair of objects.
- How do the objects "fish" and "sea" go together?

Fishes move by swimming in the sea.

- Now, look at the object "bird".
- Which of the possible choices follows the previous rule?

Birds move by flying in the sky, so the correct answer is A.

Tips for Solving Picture Analogies

- Try to identify the correlation between the first two pictures.

- Review all answers before you make a choice.

- The best approach to answering questions that might seem difficult is to proceed by elimination. Only one of the given answers will be correct. In case of doubt, find out which choice is less likely to be the correct one and eliminate it. This way of proceeding will leave fewer options and make it easier to find the right one.

- Evaluate the possible alternative uses of the objects.

- Try to transform analogies into sentences that have a logical meaning.

- Finally, the best way to improve the resolution of verbal analogies is through practice.

1.

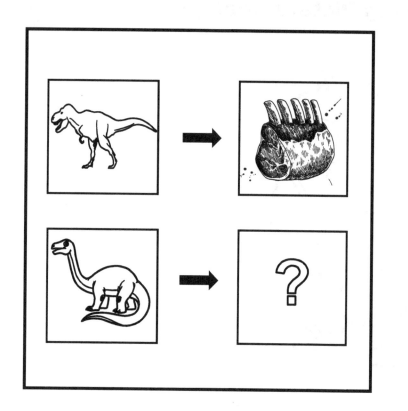

A

B

C

2.

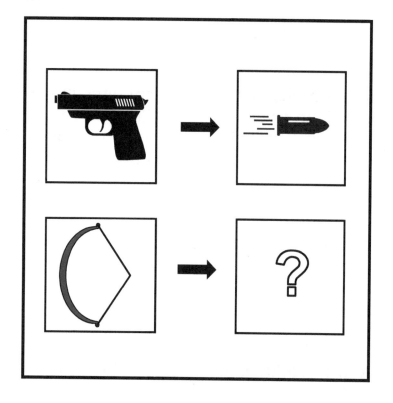

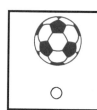

A

B

C

3

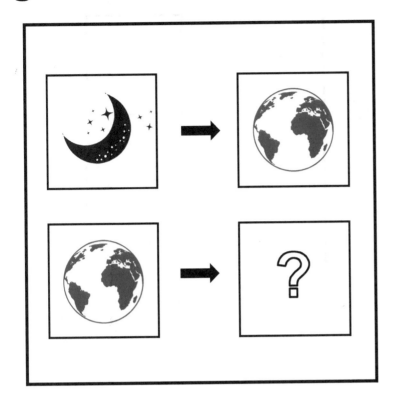

 **A**

 **B**

 **C**

4.

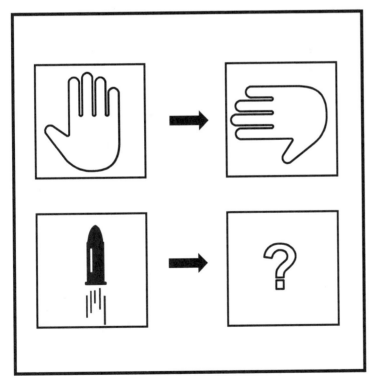

 **A**

 **B**

 **C**

5.

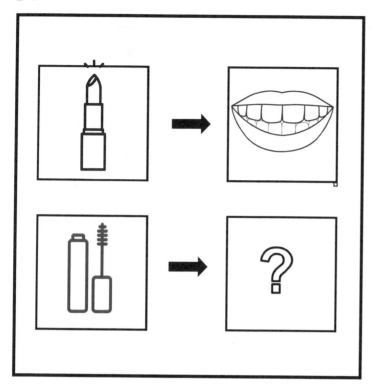

 A

 B

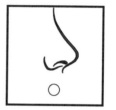 C

6.

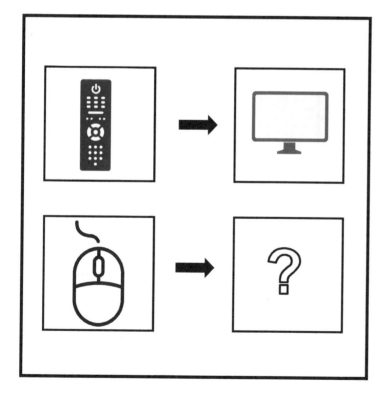

 A

 B

 C

7.

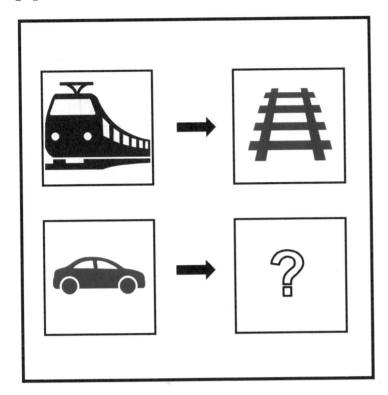

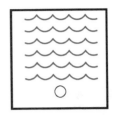 **A**

 **B**

 **C**

8.

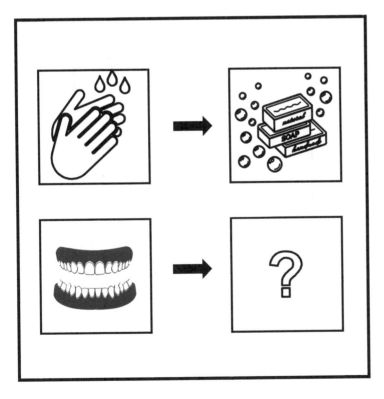

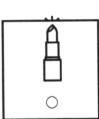 **A**

 **B**

 **C**

9.

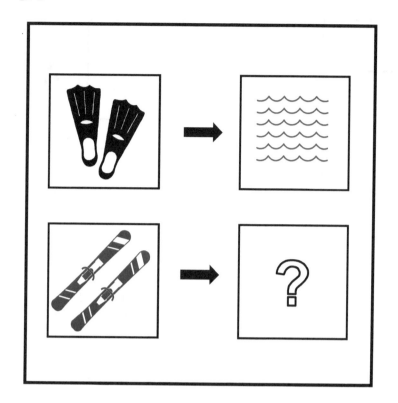

 **A**

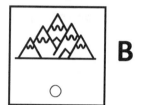 **B**

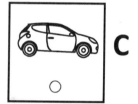 **C**

10.

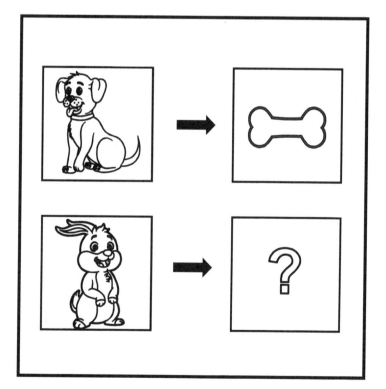

 **A**

 **B**

 **C**

11.

 **A**

 **B**

 **C**

12.

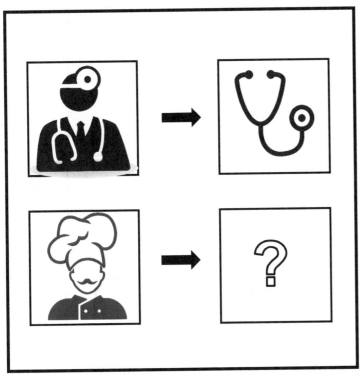

 **A**

 **B**

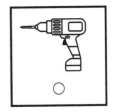 **C**

13.

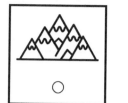 **A**

 **B**

 **C**

14.

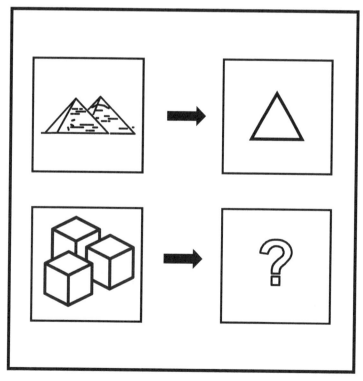

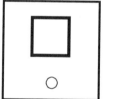 **A**

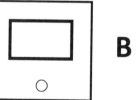 **B**

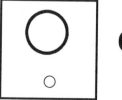 **C**

15.

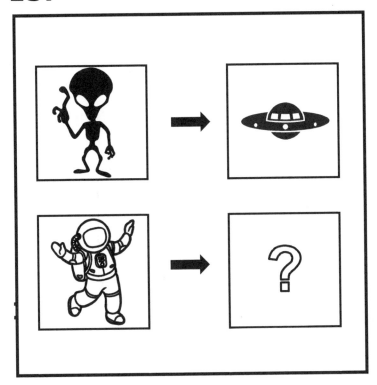

 **A**

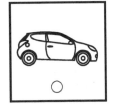 **B**

 **C**

16.

 **A**

 **B**

 **C**

Picture Classification

Picture classification questions ask the student to choose the picture that belongs to a group of three images.

Example

A   **B**   **C**

- First, identify the relationship between the three pictures in the first row.
- What do the objects "rhinoceros", "sheep", and "tiger" have in common?

Rhinoceros, sheep, and tiger are all animals.

- Now, look at the three pictures in the lower row: cat, banana, and tree. Which picture goes best with the three images in the top row?

Cat is also an animal, so the correct answer is A.

Tips for Solving Picture Classification Questions

- Try to identify the correlation between the three pictures in the top row.

- Review all answers before you make a choice.

- Remove the pictures in the answers that don't have any kind of relationship with the three pictures in the top row.

- When you work on questions, always dedicate some time to review the incorrect answers. You will learn more from them than from the correct answers.

- Encourage your child to learn how to classify and sort toys, leaves, fruits or other objects into "similar" groups.

1.

 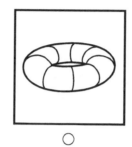 

○   ○   ○

A   **B**   **C**

2.

○   ○   ○

A   **B**   **C**

3.

  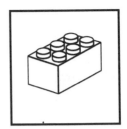

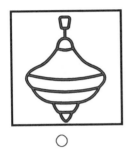  

     ○   ○   ○

     A   **B**   **C**

4.

  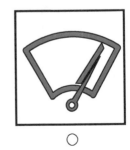

     ○   ○   ○

     A   **B**   **C**

5.

A   B   C

6.

A   B   C

7.

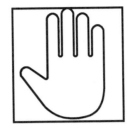  

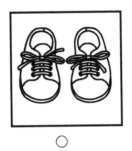 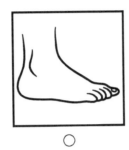 

○   ○   ○

A   **B**   **C**

8.

 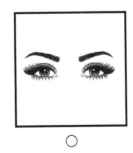 

○   ○   ○

A   **B**   **C**

9.

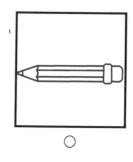

○   ○   ○

A   B   C

10.

○   ○   ○

A   B   C

11.

○ ○ ○

A **B** **C**

12.

○ ○ ○

A **B** **C**

13.

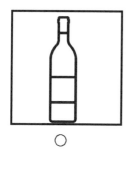  

○ ○ ○

A **B** **C**

14.

○ ○ ○

A **B** **C**

15.

○   ○   ○

A   **B**   **C**

16.

  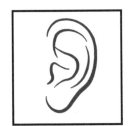

 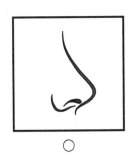 

○   ○   ○

A   **B**   **C**

Sentence Completion

The teacher reads aloud a question and does not repeat it a second time. Children must choose the picture that best answers the question in a complete, logical way.

To answer correctly, the child must be very focused on the meaning of the sentence as a whole.

Example

Which tool is needed to make a hole in the wall?

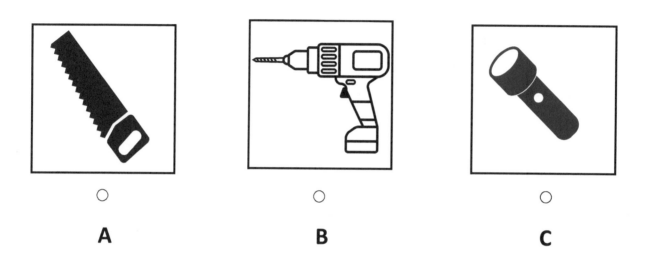

○   ○   ○

A   **B**   **C**

- First, think about the meaning of the sentence as a whole.
- Look at the answer choices.
- Try to see these tools in your mind as they are used in everyday life.

The only tool you can use to make a hole in the wall is the drill. Therefore, the right choice is "B".

Tips for Sentence Completion

- First, listen carefully to the sentence.
- Look at the three pictures in the answer row.
- Remove the pictures that don't have any kind of relationship with the main sentence.
- Try to see objects with your mind, placing them in the real world.

Directions for Sentence Completion

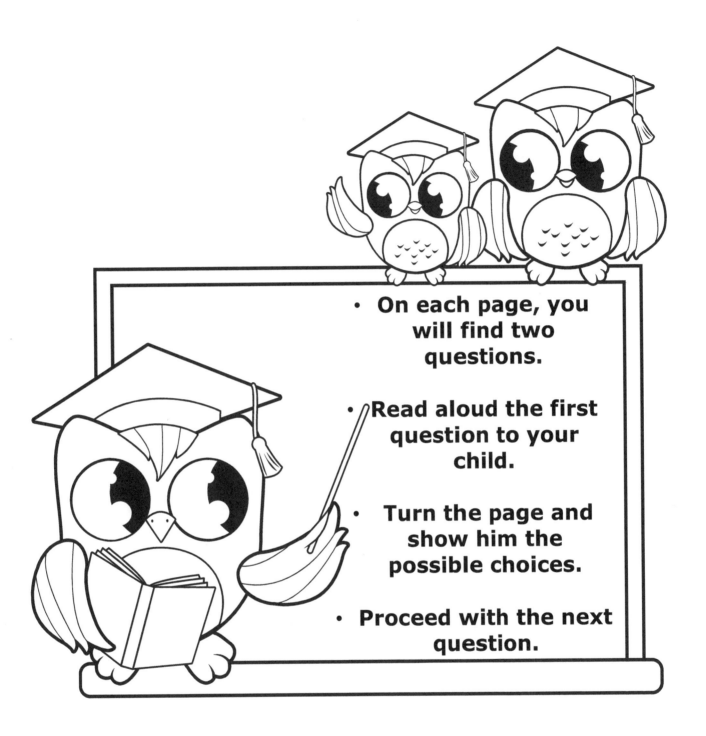

- On each page, you will find two questions.

- Read aloud the first question to your child.

- Turn the page and show him the possible choices.

- Proceed with the next question.

1.

Which tool can be used to cut a log?

2.

Which object could you sit on?

1.

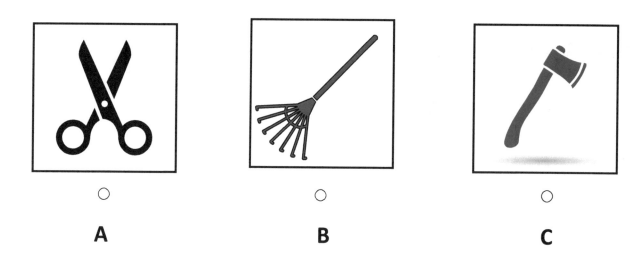

A   B   C

2.

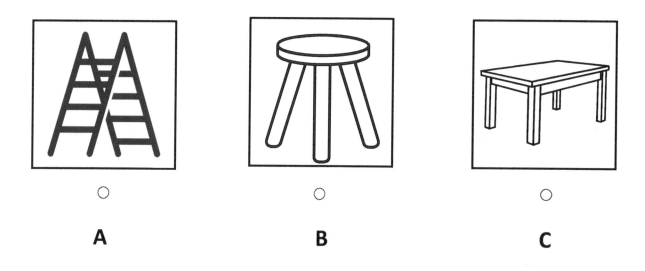

A   B   C

3.

Which one of these objects will not be found in a kitchen?

4.

Which image shows a reptile?

3.

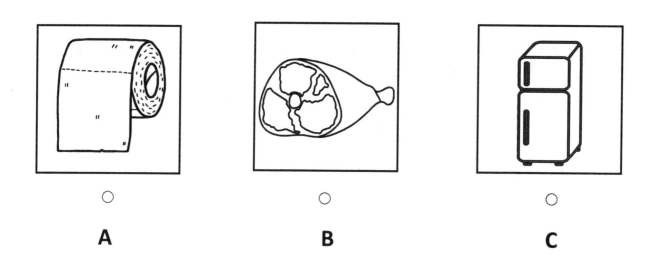

A   B   C

4

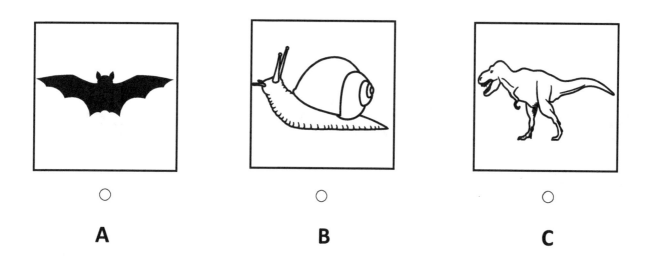

A   B   C

5.

Mary wants to take his dog for a walk. Which one of these objects will she use?

6.

Which one of these pictures does not show a wild animal?

5.

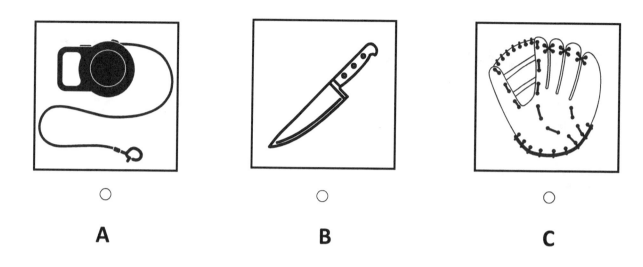

A   B   C

6.

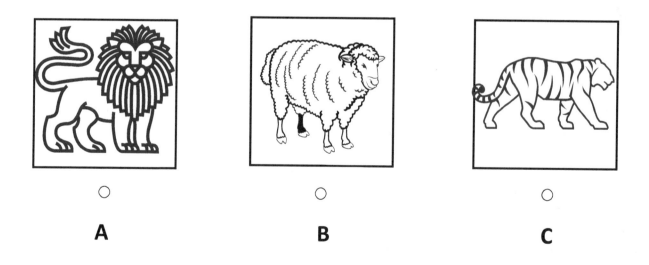

A   B   C

7.

Mary's dad is a chef. Which one of these images shows Mary's dad at work?

8.

Which one of these images shows less than four fruits?

7.

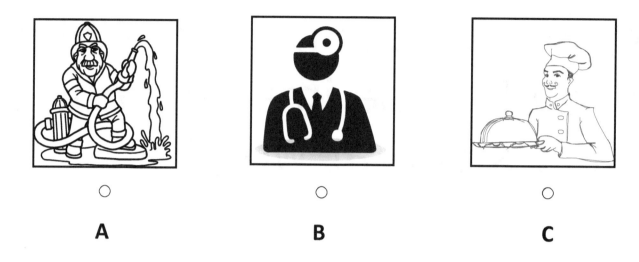

A B C

8.

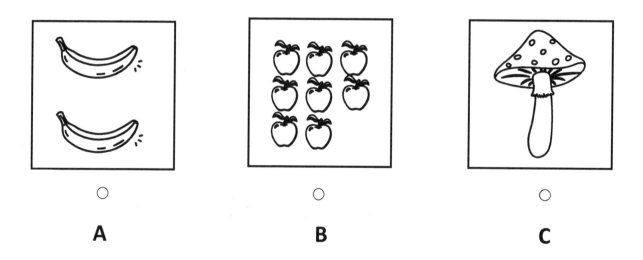

A B C

9.

Mom is making a birthday cake. Which ingredient will she not need?

10.

Which one of these images shows an apple on a table?

9.

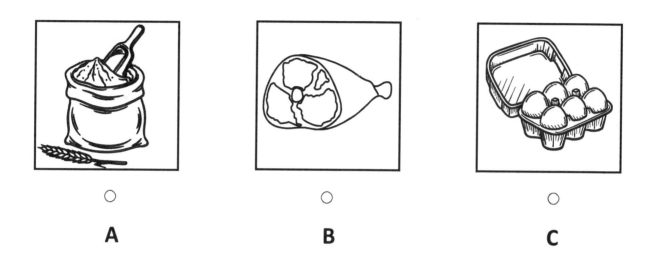

A   B   C

10.

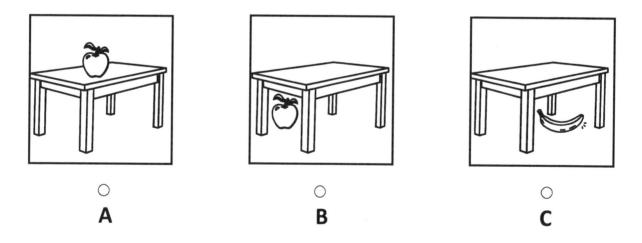

A   B   C

11.

It's raining. Mike wants to go out for a walk. Which of the following items will he not need?

12.

Which of these pictures does not show a part of a house?

11.

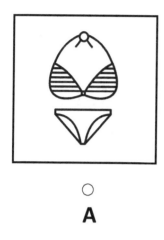

○
A

○
B

○
C

12.

○
A

○
B

○
C

13.

Oscar wants to go camping with friends. Which object will he not need?

14.

Which of these images does not show a jumping animal?

13.

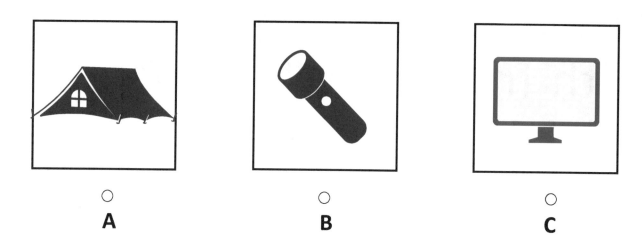

A   B   C

14.

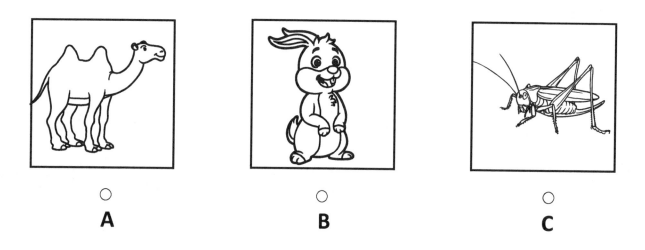

A   B   C

15.

Which fruit is needed for making wine?

16.

Mary is going to Africa. Which animal will she not meet?

15.

○
A

○
B

○
C

16.

○
A

○
B

○
C

PRACTICE TEST NON VERBAL BATTERY

This section is designed to assess a student's ability to reason and think beyond what they've already been taught. This section includes geometric shapes and figures that aren't normally seen in the classroom.

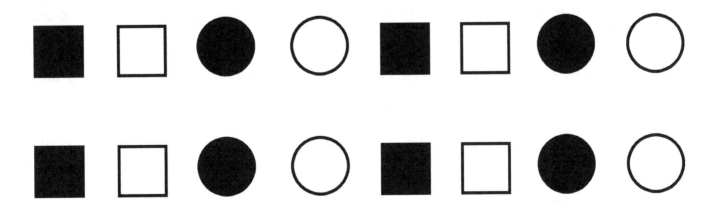

Figure Matrices

Children are provided with a 2X2 matrix with the image missing in one cell. They have to identify the relationship between the two spatial shapes in the upper line and find a fourth image that has the same correlation with the left shape in the lower line.

Example

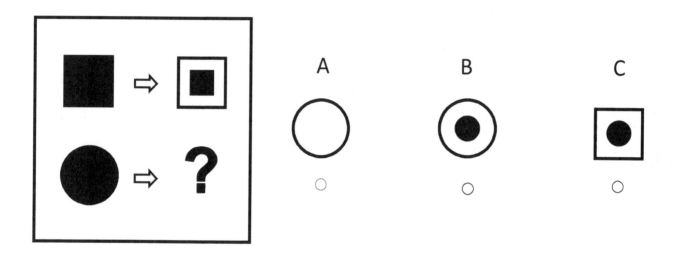

In the upper left box, the image shows a black square. In the upper right box, the image shows the same square, but in white color with a little black square inside.

The lower left box shows a black circle. Which answer choice would go with this image in the same way as the upper images go together?

The image of the answer choice must show a circle but in white color with a little black circle inside, following the same logic of the upper shapes.
The right answer is "B".

Tips for Figure Matrices

- Consider all the answer choices before selecting one.

- Try to use logic and sequential reasoning.

- Eliminate the logically wrong answers to restrict the options.

- Train yourself to decipher the relationship between different figures and shapes.

- Try using real shapes to better understand their relationships and similarities.

1.

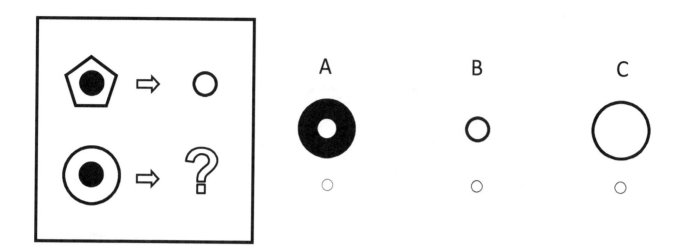

2.

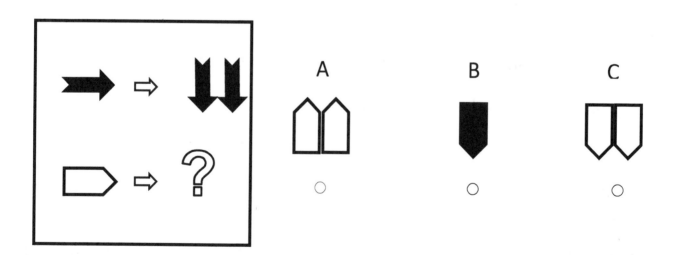

3.

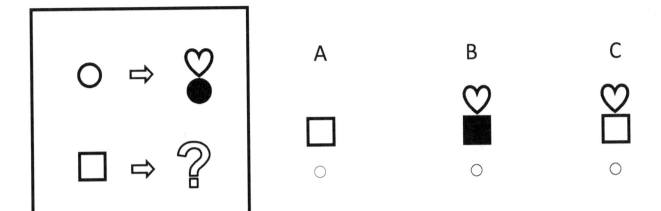

4.

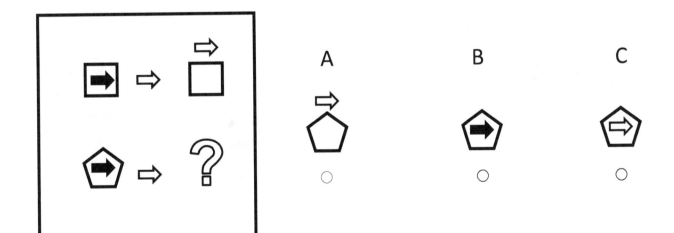

5.

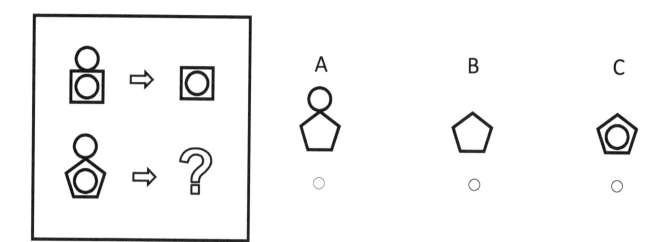

6.

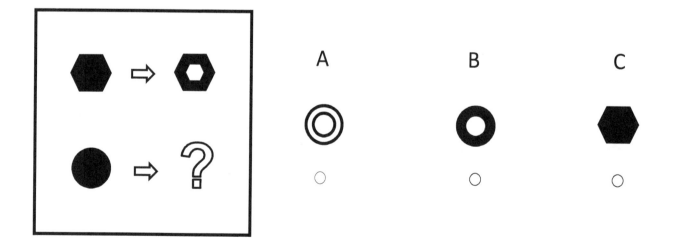

7.

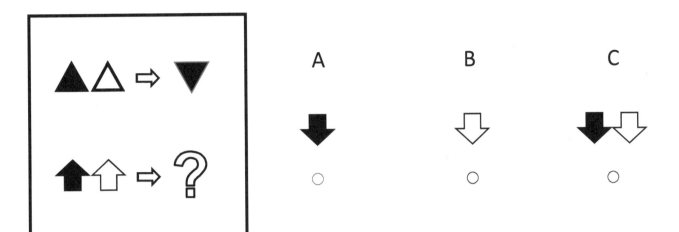

8.

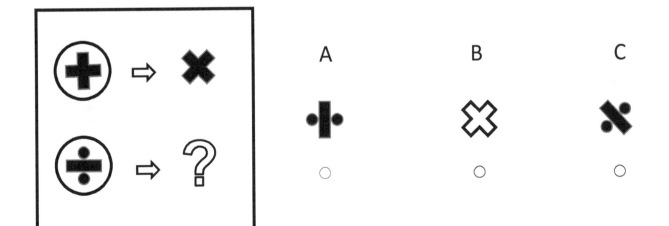

9.

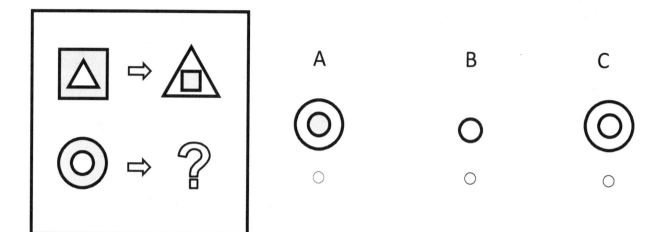

10.

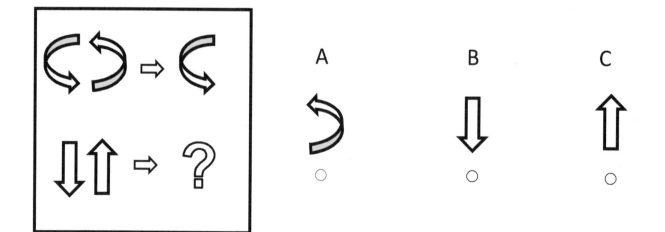

11.

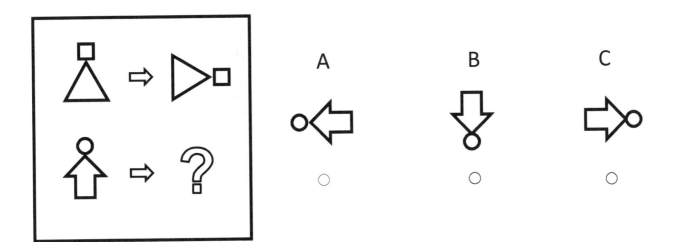

12.

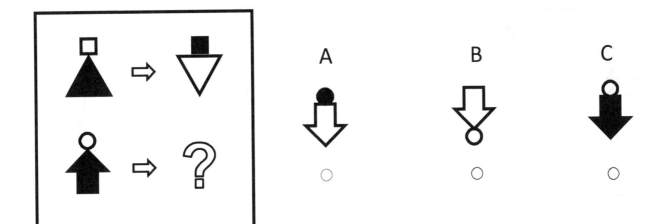

13.

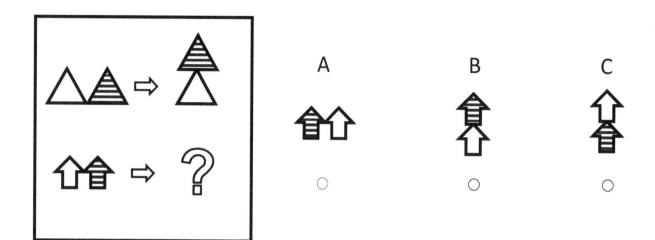

A   B   C

14.

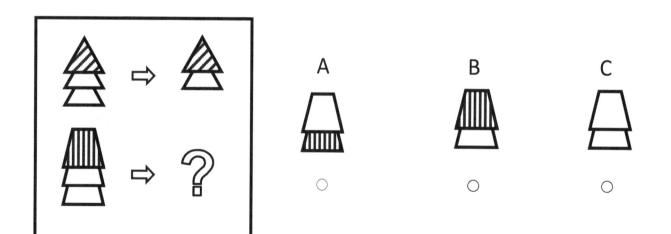

A   B   C

15.

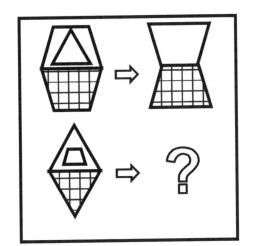

A	B	C

16.

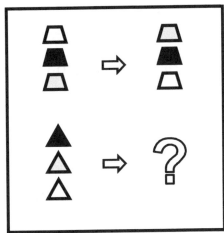

A	B	C
	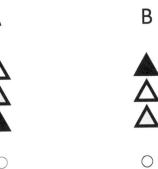	

Figure Classification

Students are provided with three shapes and they have to select the answer choice that should be the fourth figure in the set, based on the similarity with the other three figures. The intention is to test the student's ability to recognize similar patterns and to make a rational choice.

Example

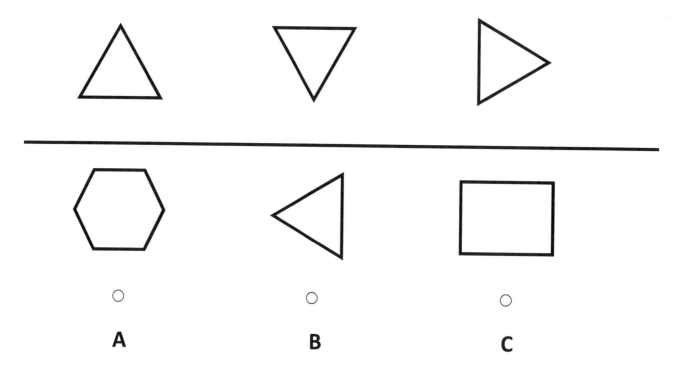

A   **B**   **C**

Look at the three pictures on the top. What do these three figures have in common?

You can see three white triangles in the same size.

Now, look at the shapes in the row of the answer choices. Which image matches best the three shapes in the top row?

The image of the answer choice must be a white triangle. The right answer is "B".

Tips for Figure Classification

- Be sure to review all answer choices before selecting one.

- Try to use logic and sequential reasoning.

- Carefully consider the elements of each figure:

1. color
2. form
3. number of sides
4. orientation
5. number of elements inside each figure

- Try to exclude the obviously wrong options to reduce the answer choices.

1.

○   ○   ○

A   **B**   **C**

2.

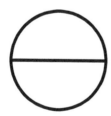  

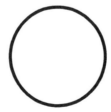 

○   ○   ○

A   **B**   **C**

3.

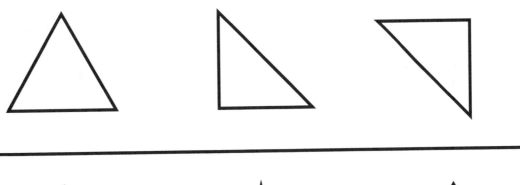

      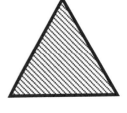

○   ○   ○

A   **B**   **C**

4.

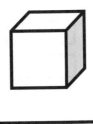

○   ○   ○

A   **B**   **C**

5.

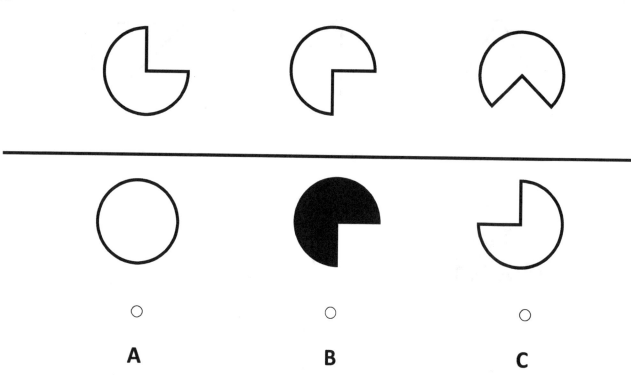

A   **B**   **C**

6.

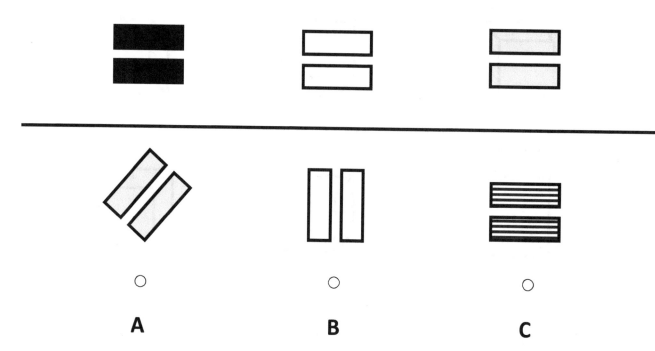

A   **B**   **C**

7.

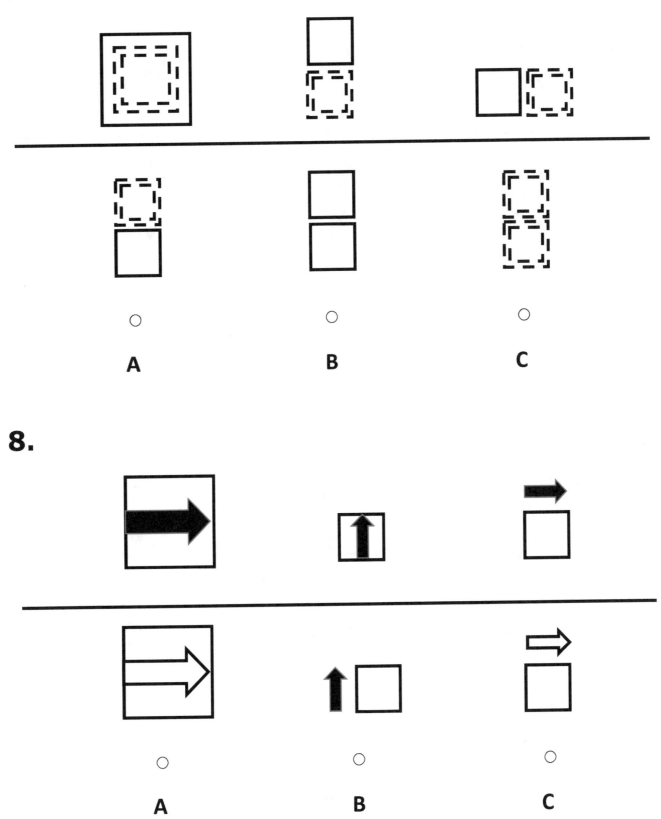

A   B   C

8.

A   B   C

9.

○ ○ ○

A **B** **C**

10.

○ ○ ○

A **B** **C**

11.

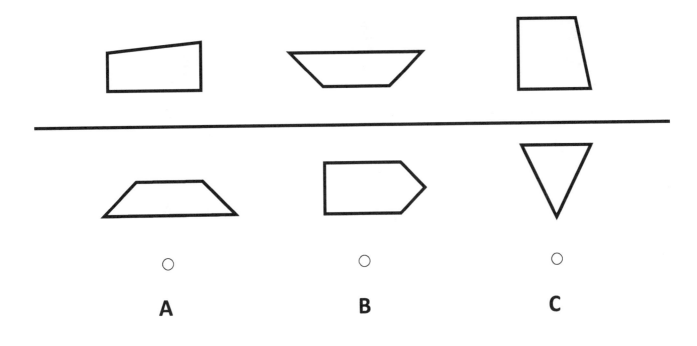

A   B   C

12.

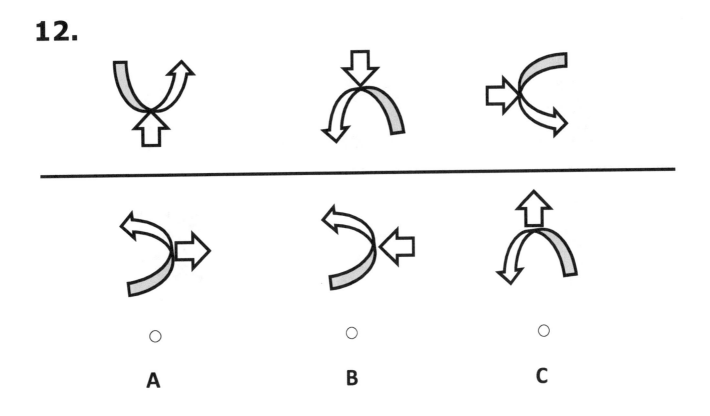

A   B   C

13.

○   ○   ○

A   **B**   **C**

14.

○   ○   ○

A   **B**   **C**

15.

○ A   ○ B   ○ C

16.

○ A   ○ B   ○ C

Paper Folding

Children need to determine the appearance of a perforated and folded sheet of paper, once opened.

Example

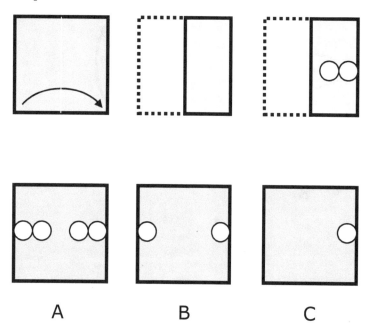

A   B   C

The figures at the top represent a square piece of paper being folded, and the last of these figures has two holes on it.

One of the lower three figures shows where the perforations will be when the paper is fully unfolded. You have to understand which of these images is the right one.

First, the paper was folded horizontally, from left to right.

Then, two holes was punched out. Therefore, when the paper is unfolded the holes will mirror on the left and right side of the sheet. The right answer is "A".

Tips for Paper Folding

The best way to get ready for these challenging questions is to practice. The patterns that show up on the test can confuse students, so the demonstration of folding and unfolding real paper can be very helpful.

1.

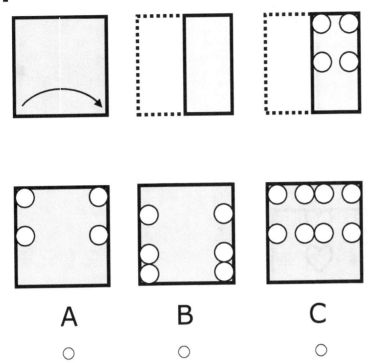

A   B   C

○   ○   ○

2.

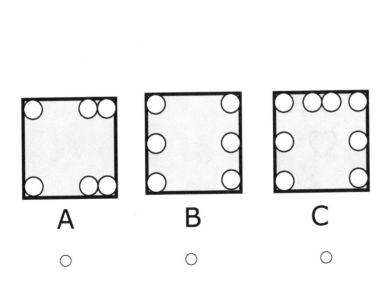

A   B   C

○   ○   ○

3.

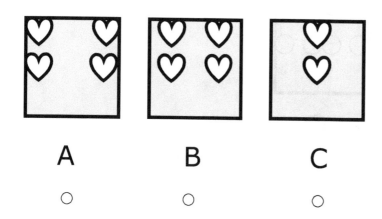

A   B   C

○   ○   ○

4.

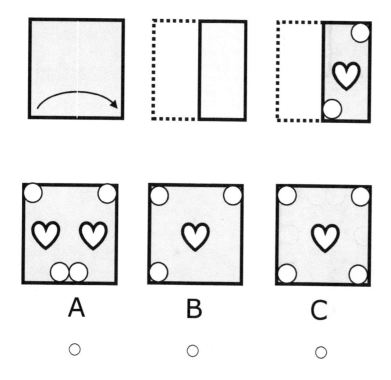

A   B   C

○   ○   ○

5.

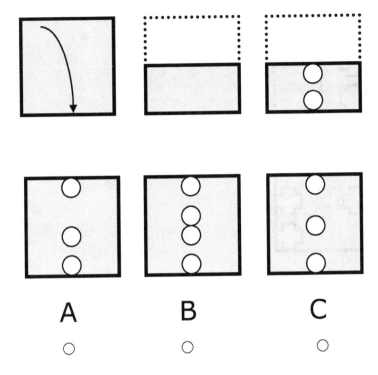

A   B   C

○   ○   ○

6.

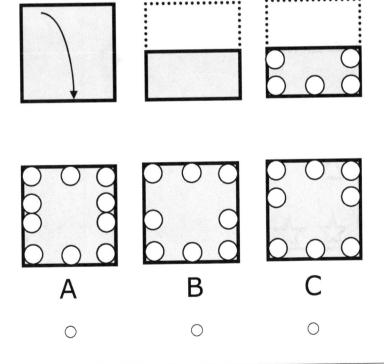

A   B   C

○   ○   ○

7.

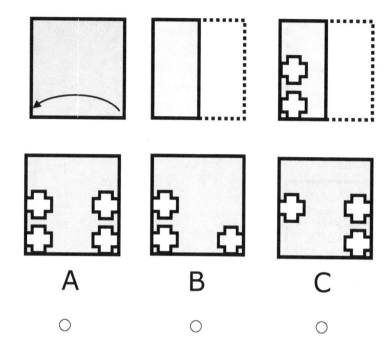

A   B   C

○   ○   ○

8.

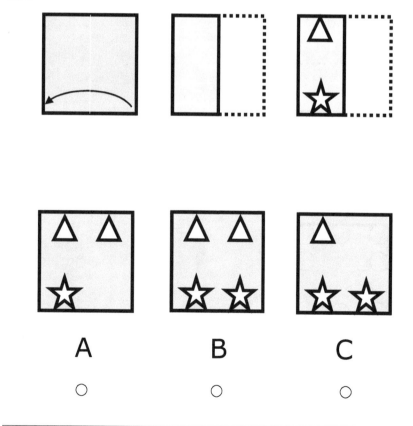

A   B   C

○   ○   ○

9.

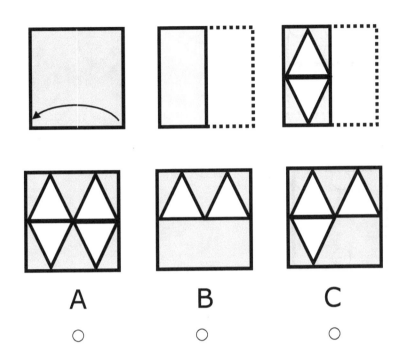

A ○   B ○   C ○

10.

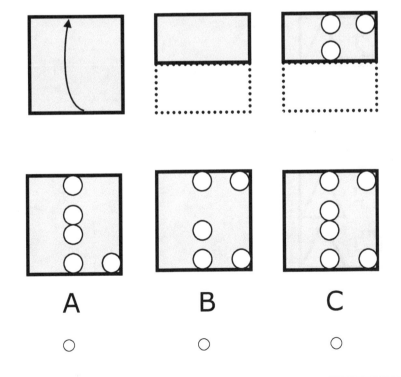

A ○   B ○   C ○

11.

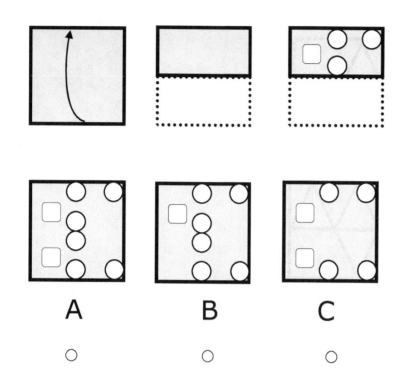

A   B   C

○   ○   ○

12.

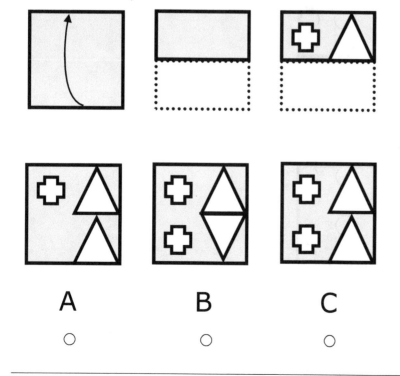

A   B   C

○   ○   ○

PRACTICE TEST QUANTITATIVE BATTERY

This section introduces abstract reasoning and problem-solving skills to learners and is one of the most challenging sections in the test.

Number Puzzle

Children see two trains. They must choose the answer picture that makes the second train carrying an equal number of things as the first one.

Example

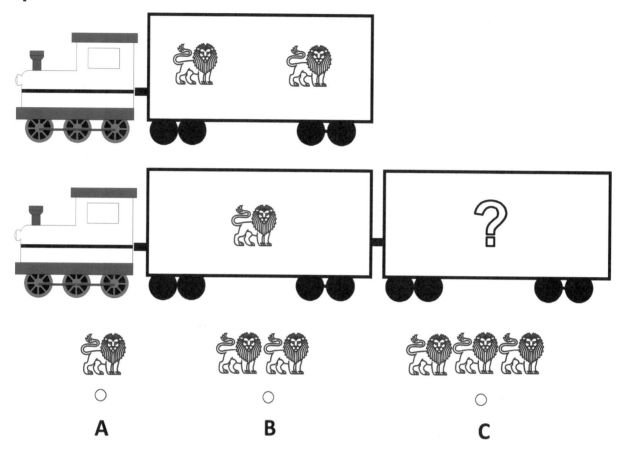

- Look at the train in the top row. In this train, there are 2 lions. In the train on the bottom row, there are 1 lion in one wagon.
- How many lions are needed in the wagon with the question mark, so that both trains have the same amount of lions?
- 1 lion is needed to make a total of 2 lions in the bottom train.
- The correct answer is A

Tips for Number Puzzle

- Try to fully understand the meaning of "equal", as the purpose is to provide the missing items that will make the 2 trains carry the same number of objects.
- Train yourself to solve simple additions and subtractions.
- Work with real objects to understand the concepts.

1.

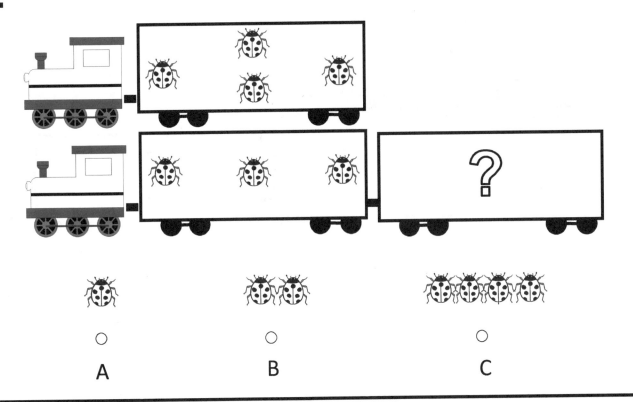

A   B   C

2.

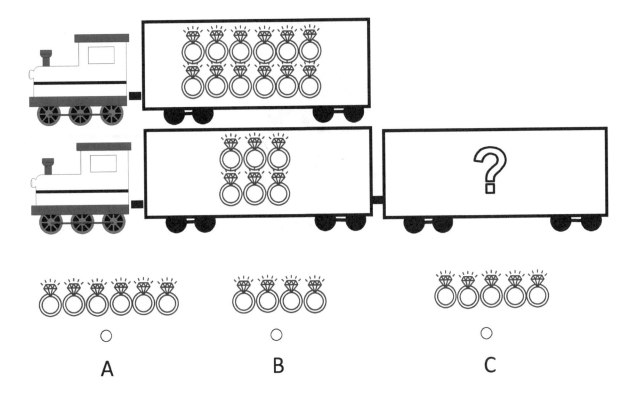

A   B   C

3.

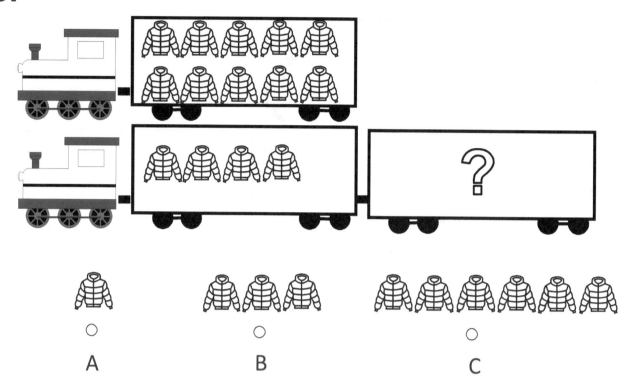

A   B   C

4.

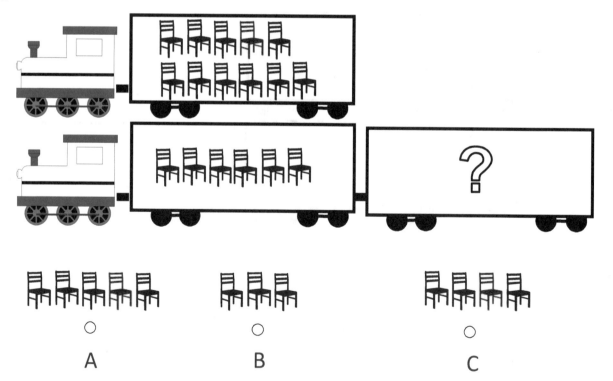

A   B   C

5.

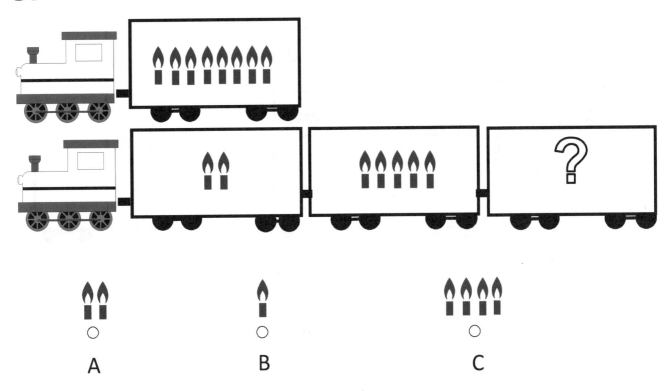

A   B   C

6.

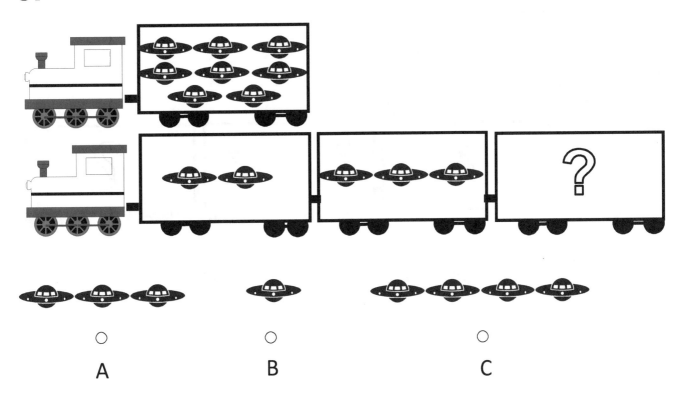

A   B   C

7.

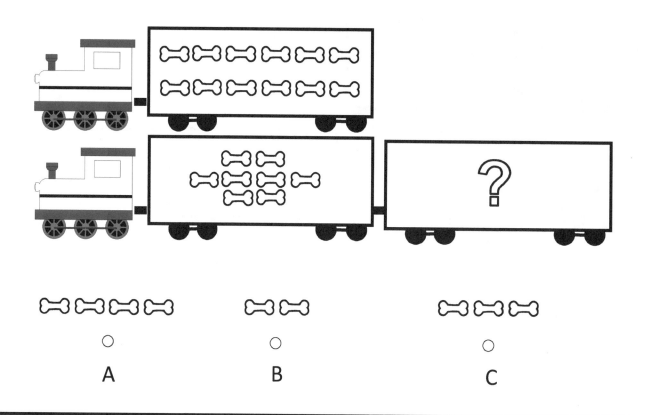

A   B   C

8.

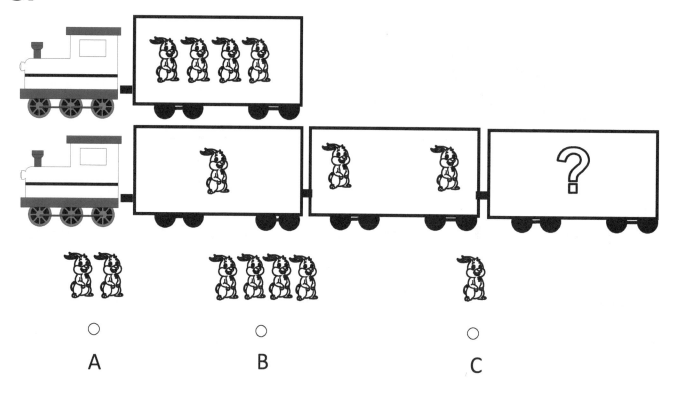

A   B   C

9.

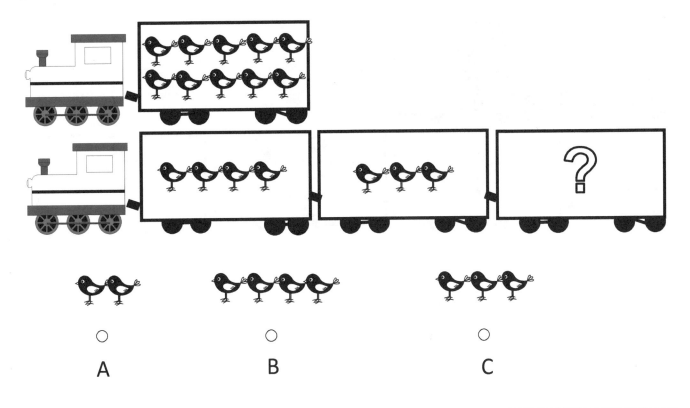

A   B   C

10.

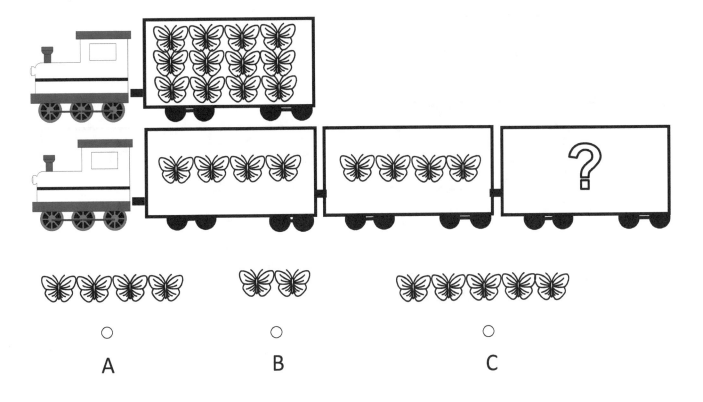

A   B   C

11.

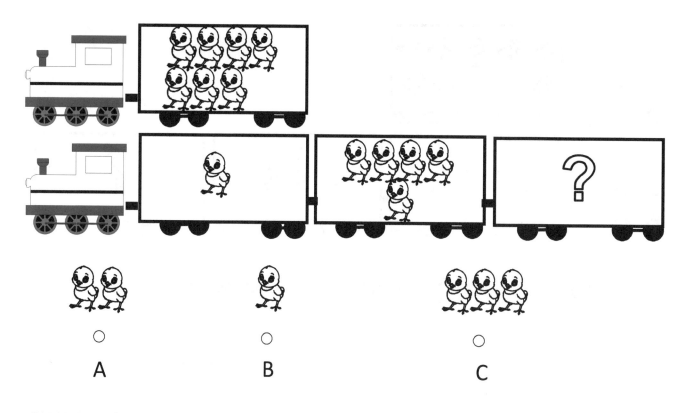

A   B   C

12.

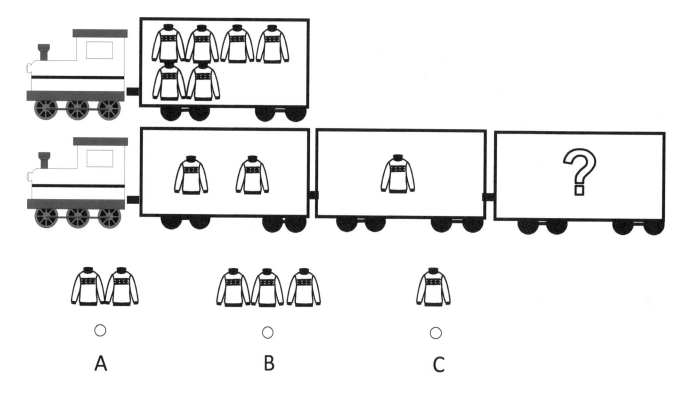

A   B   C

Number Analogies

Children will be provided with 2x2 basic matrices. Each box of the matrices contains a certain number of objects. In the lower row, the child must identify the same relationship as in the upper row and select the answer option that best fits the box with the question mark.

Example

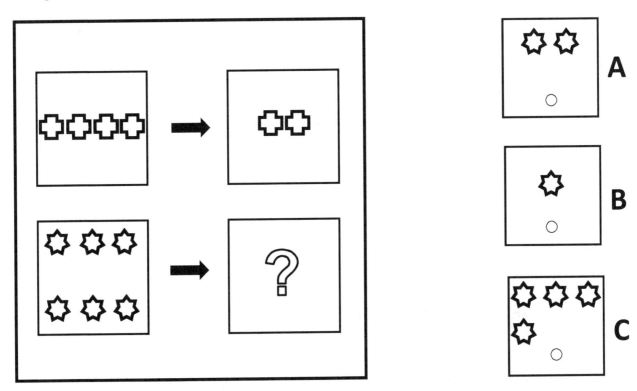

- First, identify the relationship between the objects in the upper squares.

  What is the relationship between "4 cross" and "2 cross"?

  4 is greater than 2 by 2 (4-2=2).

- Now, look at the objects in the lower squares. In the left box we have 6 stars.
- Which of the possible choices follows the previous rule?

  In the right box, we should have 2 less stars. Therefore, the correct answer is C (6-2=4).

Tips for Number Analogies

- Step 1: Acquire all the information from the two given pairs (relationships, sums, subtractions, etc.).

- Step 2: Apply the same rules, relations, formulas that you correctly identified in step 1.

- Step 3: Double-check that the rule has been properly applied.

- Train yourself to solve simple additions and subtractions.

- Work with real objects to understand the concepts.

- Start with simple numerical analogies and gradually increase the level of complexity.

1.

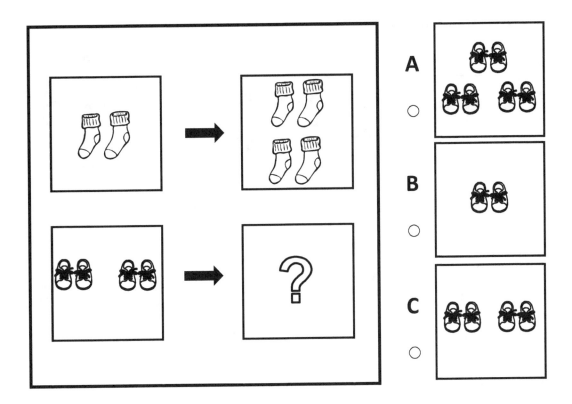

2.

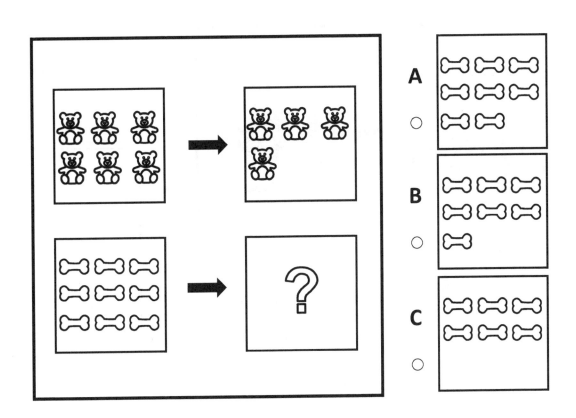

3.

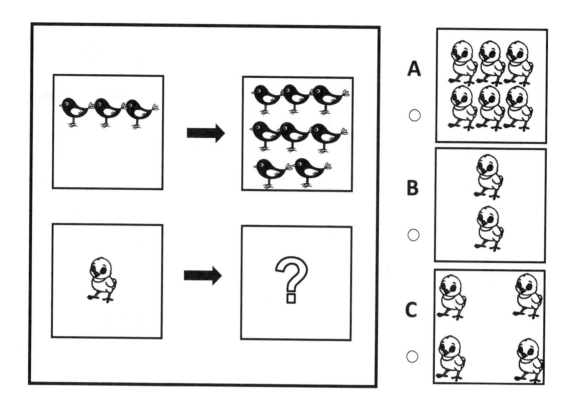

4.

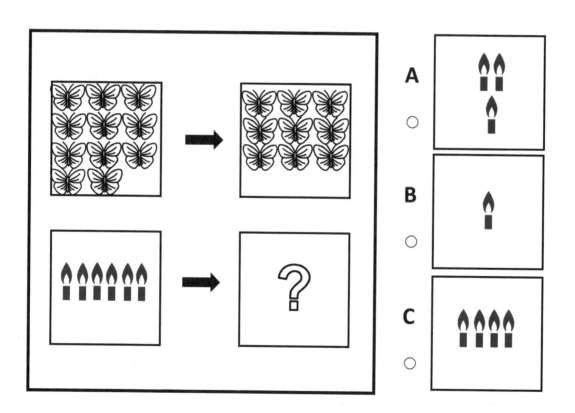

5.

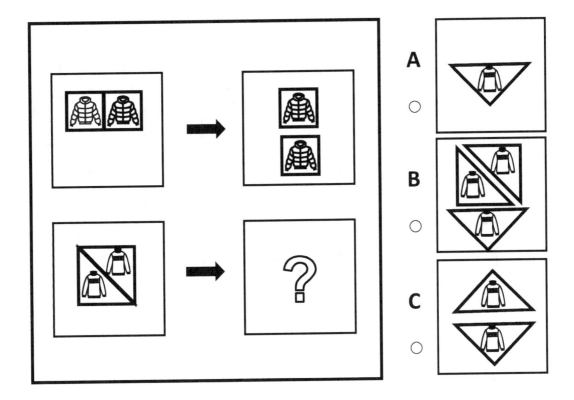

6.

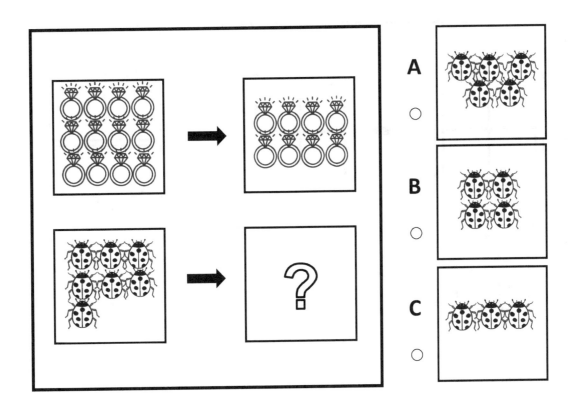

7.

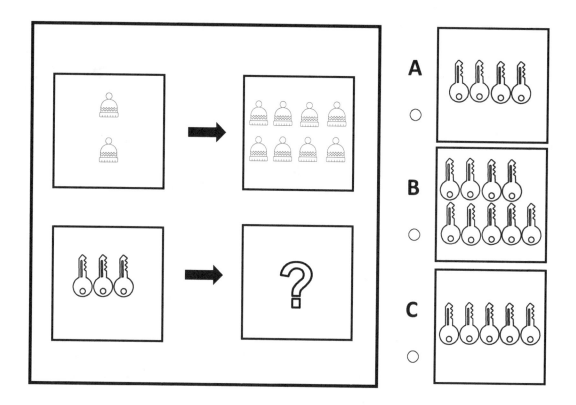

8.

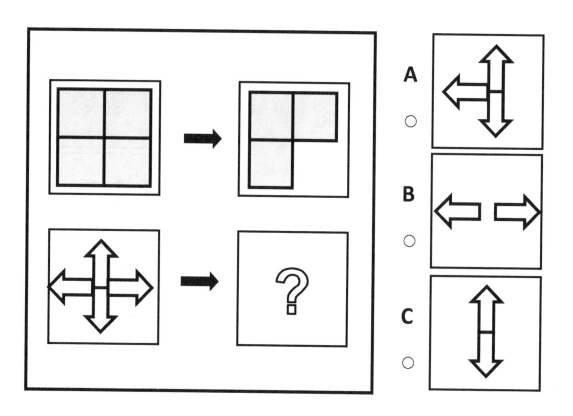

9.

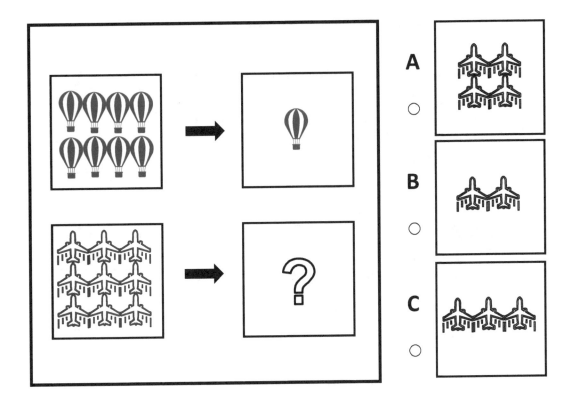

10.

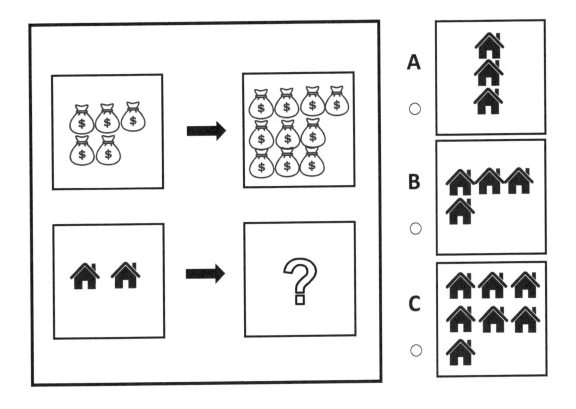

11.

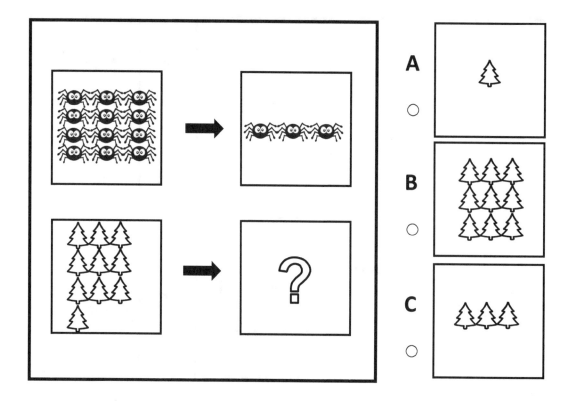

A ◯

B ◯

C ◯

12.

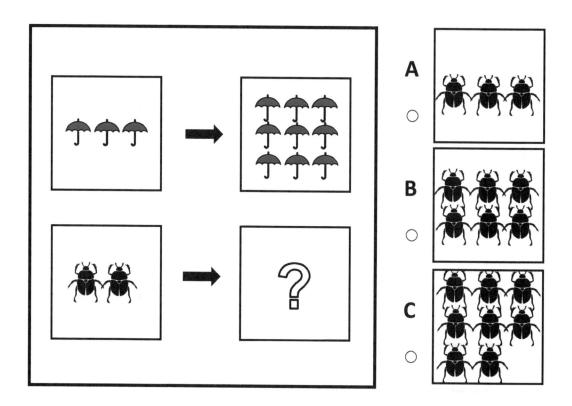

A ◯

B ◯

C ◯

13.

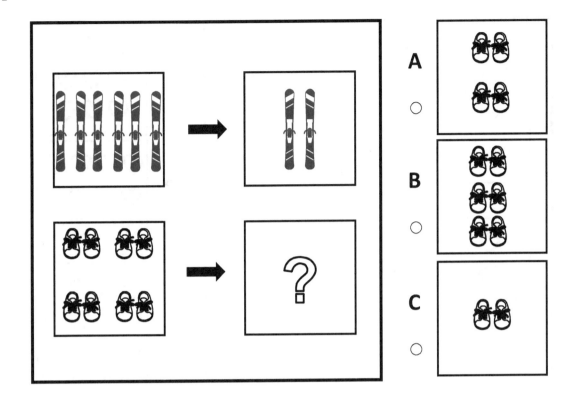

14.

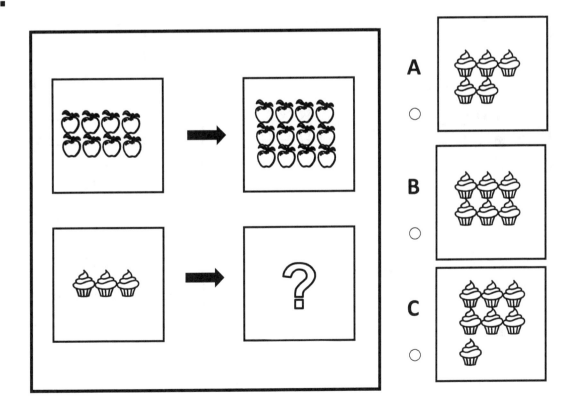

15.

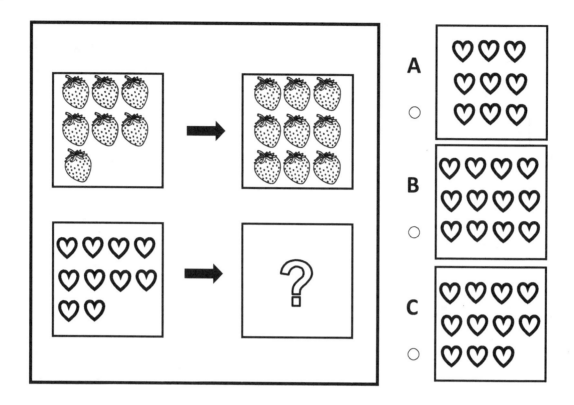

16.

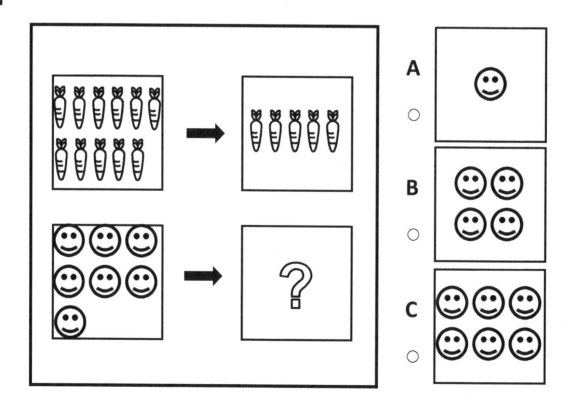

Number Series

Children are required to determine which string of beads is needed to complete a sequence that follows a specific pattern by observing an abacus.

Example 1

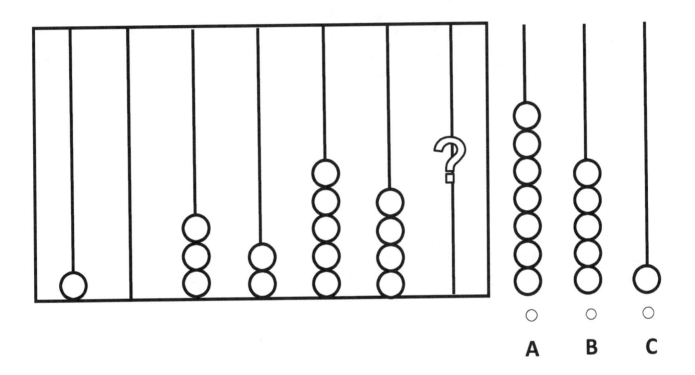

- The numbers on the strings are: 1   0   3   2   5   4   ?
- **1-1=0; 0+3=3; 3-1=2; 2+3=5; 5-1=4; etc.**
- It's easy to realize that the sequence is **-1, +3, -1, +3, -1, etc.**
- Apply the same rule to the number 4.

4 + 3 = 7 The right answer is "A"

Example 2

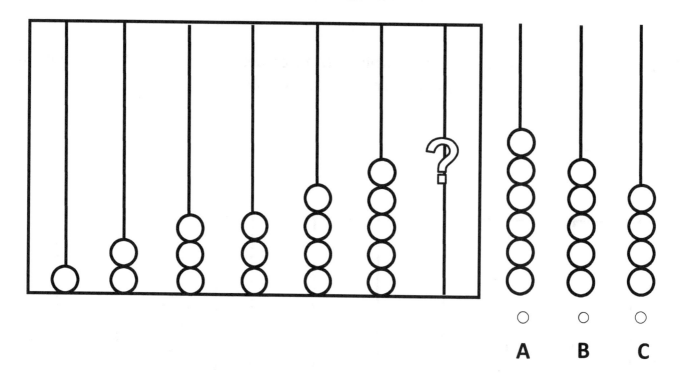

.

- The numbers on the strings are: 1   2   3   3   4   5   ?
- 1+**1**=2; 2+**1**=3; 3+**0**=3; 3+**1**=4; 4+**1**=5 etc.
- It's easy to realize that the sequence is: +1, +1, 0, +1, +1, 0, etc.
- Apply the same rule to the number 5.

5+0=5 The right answer is "B"

Tips for Number Series

To answer these questions, children will need to be able to identify the pattern in a sequence of numbers and provide the missing item. Therefore, it is necessary to perform as many exercises as possible, moving from the easiest to the hardest.

In the beginning, to make the logic of the sequences easier, it is useful to work with real objects.

1

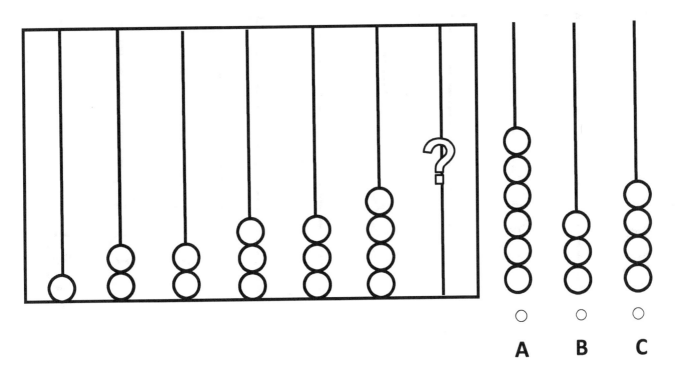

2.

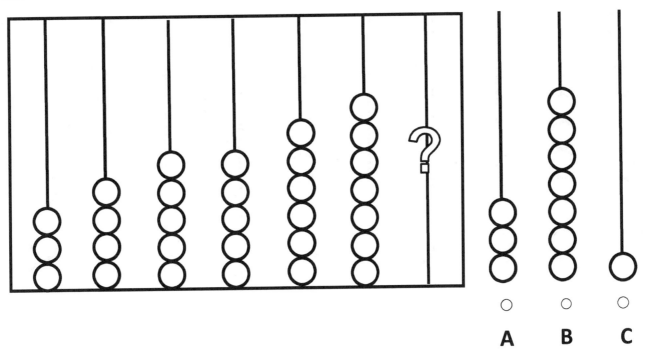

3.

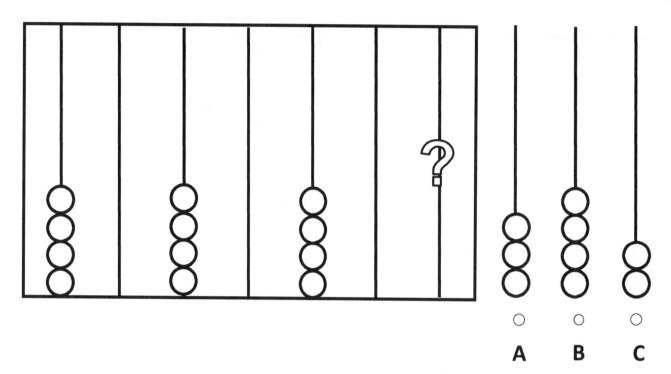

A B C

4.

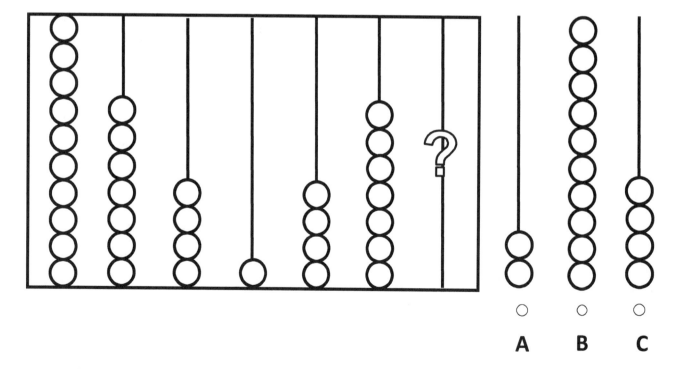

A B C

5.

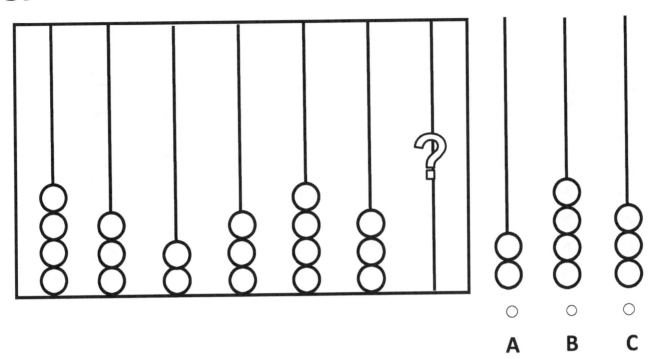

6.

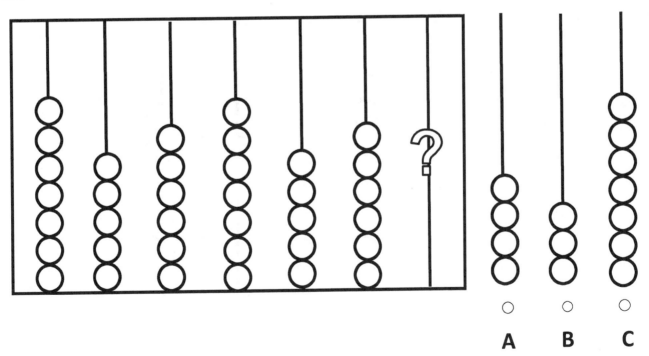

7.

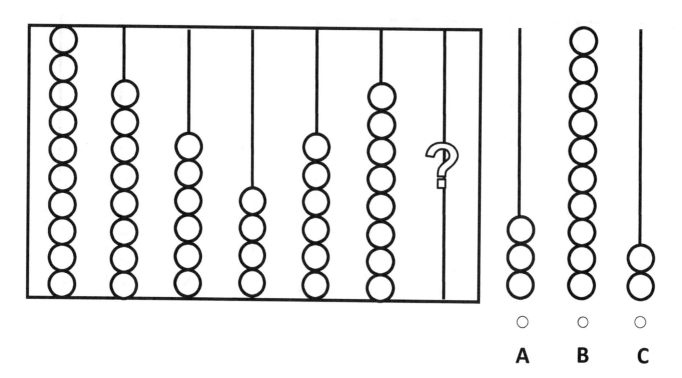

A B C

8.

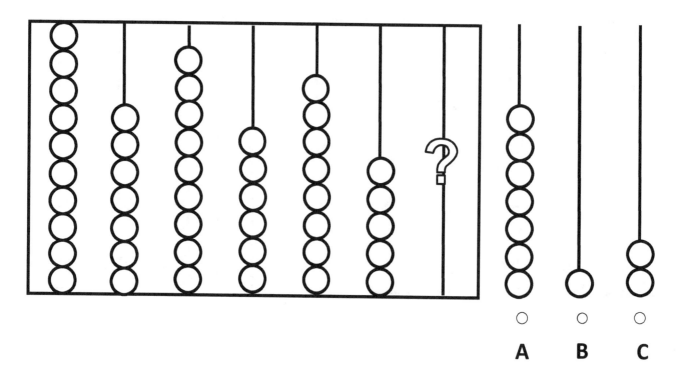

A B C

9.

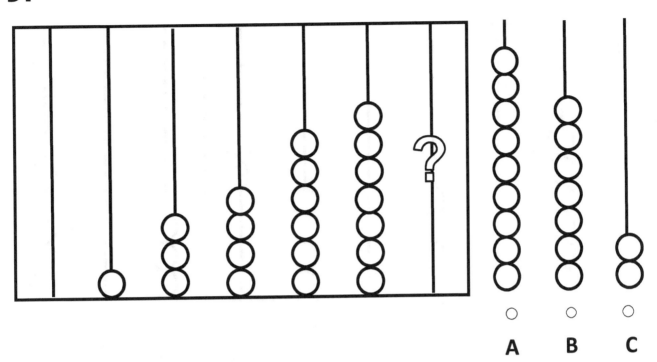

10.

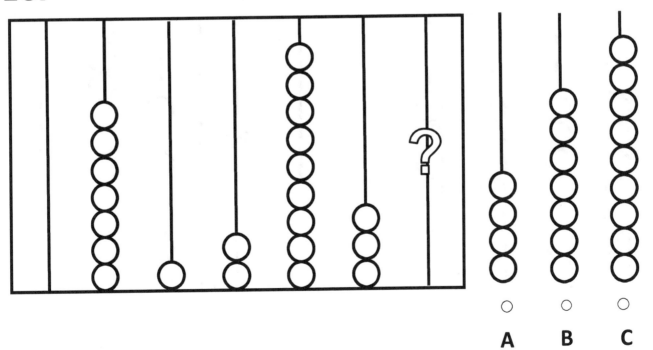

11.

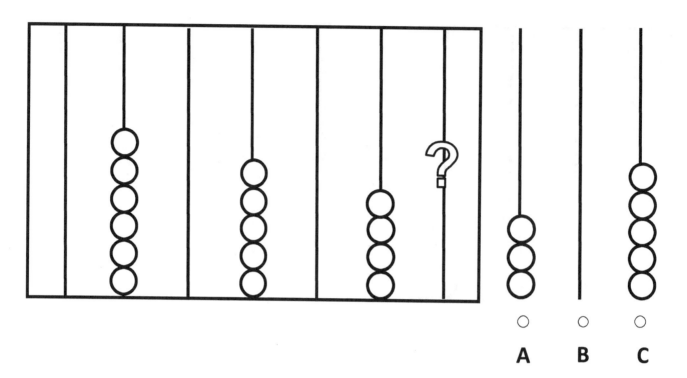

12.

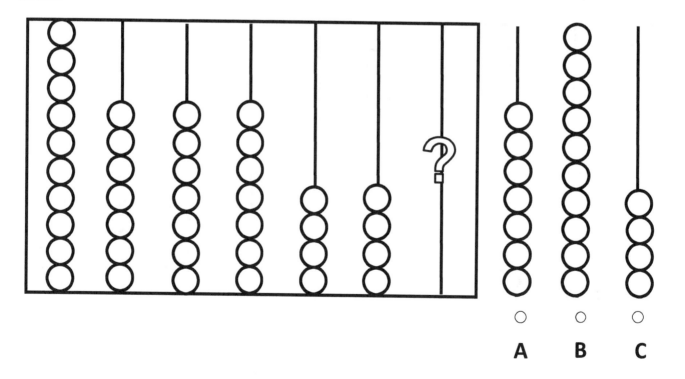

13.

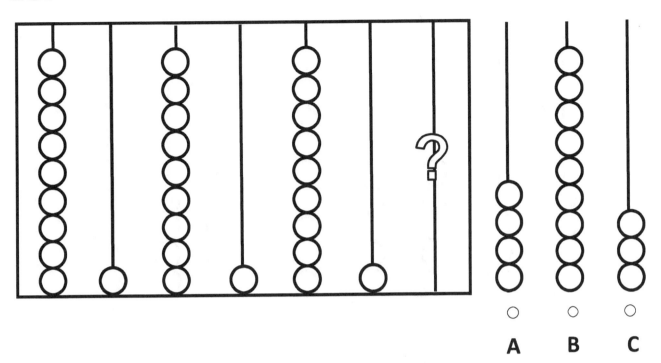

A   B   C

14.

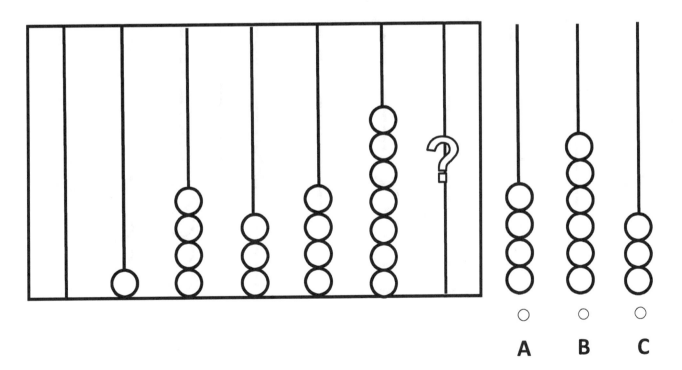

A   B   C

15.

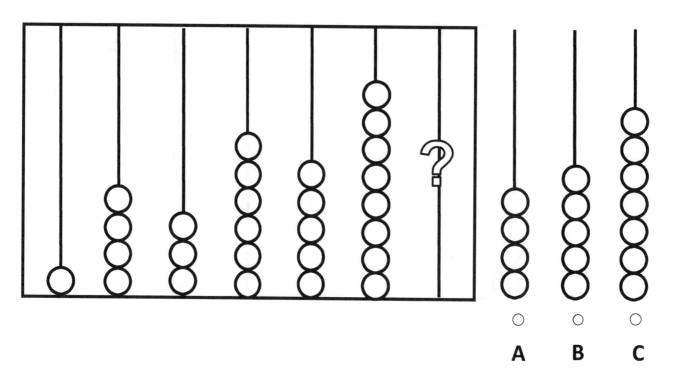

16.

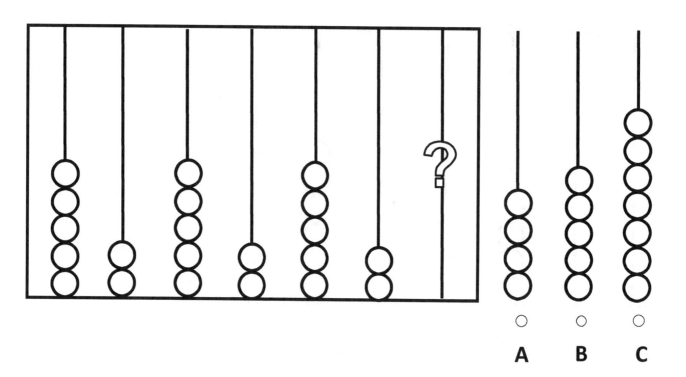

HOW TO DOWNLOAD 54 BONUS QUESTIONS

Thank you for reading this book, we hope you really enjoyed it and found it very helpful.

PLEASE LEAVE US A REVIEW ON THE WEBSITE WHERE YOU PURCHASED THIS BOOK!

By leaving a review, you give us the opportunity to improve our work.

A GIFT FOR YOU!

FREE ONLINE ACCESS TO 54 BONUS PRACTICE QUESTIONS.

Follow this link:

https://www.skilledchildren.com/free-download-cogat-test-prep-grade-1.php
You will find a PDF to download: please insert this PASSWORD: 140228

Nicole Howard and the SkilledChildren.com Team

www.skilledchildren.com

ANSWER KEY

Picture Analogies Practice Test
p.14

1.
Answer: option B
Explanation: T-Rex was a carnivorous dinosaur; Apatosaurus was an herbivorous dinosaur.

2.
Answer: option C
Explanation: Guns throw bullets; bows throw arrows.

3.
Answer: option B
Explanation: The Moon rotates around the Earth; the Earth rotates around the Sun.

4.
Answer: option A
Explanation: The figures on the left rotate by 90 degrees counterclockwise.

5.
Answer: option B
Explanation: Lipstick is for lips; mascara is for eyes.

6.
Answer: option A
Explanation: The remote control is used for the television; the mouse is used for the computer.

7.
Answer: option B
Explanation: Trains move on the rails; cars move on the road.

8.
Answer: option C
Explanation: To wash your hands, you use soap; to brush your teeth, you use toothpaste.

9.

Answer: option B

Explanation: Fins are used to the sea; skis are used in the mountains.

10.

Answer: option B

Explanation: Dogs love bones; rabbits love carrots.

11.

Answer: option A

Explanation: Snowmen are made of snow; sweaters are made of wool.

12.

Answer: option A

Explanation: Doctors use stethoscopes; cooks use knives.

13.

Answer: option B

Explanation: Books are put in libraries; money is put in strongboxes.

14.

Answer: option A

Explanation: The basic shape of the Pyramid is the triangle; the basic shape of the cube is the square.

15.

Answer: option A

Explanation: The vehicle of an alien is the flying saucer; the vehicle of an astronaut is the rocket.

16.

Answer: option B

Explanation: The plug must be inserted into the socket; the key must be inserted into the lock.

Picture Classification Practice Test
p.24

1.
Answer: option B
Explanation: Swimsuit, flippers, swimming goggles and life buoy are used at the sea.

2.
Answer: option C
Explanation: Helicopters, airplanes, rockets, and hot air balloons fly in the sky.

3.
Answer: option A
Explanation: Teddy bear, rocking horse, block cube, and spinning top are children's toys.

4.
Answer: option C
Explanation: Steering wheel, tire, car key, and wiper are parts of a car.

5.
Answer: option A
Explanation: Football helmet, baseball hat, woolen hat, and chef's hat are all headgear.

6.
Answer: option B
Explanation: Eyeglasses, telescopes, cameras, and microscopes are used with the eyes.

7.
Answer: option B
Explanation: Hands, eyes, ears, and feet are parts of the body.

8.
Answer: option A
Explanation: Drums, bells, trumpets, and doorbells emit sounds.

9.
Answer: option C
Explanation: Tennis rackets, baseball bats, balls and skis are sports equipment.

10.
Answer: option B
Explanation: The drill, refrigerator, lamp, and television work with electricity.

11.
Answer: option C
Explanation: Chairs, stools, armchairs, and sleds are objects on which you can sit.

12.
Answer: option B
Explanation: Elephants, sheep, cows, and reindeer are herbivorous animals.

13.
Answer: option A
Explanation: Soup, water, milk and wine are liquids.

14.
Answer: option C
Explanation: Spider webs, nests, hives, and anthills are structures created by animals.

15.
Answer: option C
Explanation: Witches, pumpkins, bats, and ghosts are typical characters of the Halloween party.

16.
Answer: option B
Explanation: Eyes, hands, ears, and nose belong to the upper body.

Sentence Completion Practice Test

p.35

1.
Answer: option C
Explanation: Hatchet can be used to cut a log.

2.
Answer: option B
Explanation: The stool is used to sit on.

3.
Answer: option A
Explanation: Toilet paper is not stored in the kitchen.

4.
Answer: option C
Explanation: Tyrannosaurus Rex was a reptile.

5.
Answer: option A
Explanation: Mary will use a leash.

6.
Answer: option B
Explanation: Sheep is not a wild animal.

7.
Answer: option C
Explanation: Image C shows a chef at work.

8.
Answer: option A
Explanation: Image A shows less than 4 fruits. Image C does not show a fruit but a mushroom.

9.
Answer: option B
Explanation: Mommy won't need ham.

10.
Answer: option A
Explanation: Image A shows an apple on a table.

11.
Answer: option A
Explanation: Mike will not need a swimsuit.

12.
Answer: option A
Explanation: Image A does not show a part of a house but a tree.

13.
Answer: option C
Explanation: Oscar will not need television.

14.
Answer: option A
Explanation: The camel is not a jumping animal.

15.
Answer: option C
Explanation: Grape is needed to make wine.

16.
Answer: option A
Explanation: Mary will not meet a reindeer.

Figure Matrices Practice Test
p.54

1.
Answer: option B
Explanation: Larger shapes are removed; inside shapes become white.

2.
Answer: option C
Explanation: Arrows double, rotate by 90 degrees clockwise, and keep the same color as the respective figures on the left.

3.
Answer: option B
Explanation: The figure on the left turns black and a white heart appears above it.

4.
Answer: option A
Explanation: The arrow turns white and moves up over the left figure.

5.
Answer: option C
Explanation: The top circle is removed.

6.
Answer: option B
Explanation: Addiction of a smaller white shape inside the figure on the left

7.
Answer: option A
Explanation: The figure on the right disappears and the figure on the left rotates by 180 degrees clockwise.

8.
Answer: option C
Explanation: The larger figure disappears. The smaller shape rotates by 45 degrees clockwise.

9.
Answer: option A
Explanation: The larger figure becomes the smaller one and vice versa.

10.
Answer: option B
Explanation: The right arrow is removed.

11.
Answer: option C
Explanation: Both figures on the left rotate by 90 degrees clockwise.

12.
Answer: option A
Explanation: The upper shape becomes black; the lower shape becomes white and rotates by 180 degrees clockwise.

13.
Answer: option B
Explanation: The shape on the right is placed above the left one.

14.
Answer: option B
Explanation: The lower figure is removed.

15.
Answer: option C
Explanation: The shape inside the top figure is eliminated. The 2 remaining figures are overturned.

16.
Answer: option A
Explanation: The figure at the top changes place with the figure at the bottom. The figure in the middle does not move.

Figure Classification Practice Test
p.64

1.
Answer: option A
Explanation: Arrows in the same size, pointing down.

2.
Answer: option A
Explanation: Circles are divided into two equal parts.

3.
Answer: option B
Explanation: White triangles.

4.
Answer: option C
Explanation: Cubes of the same size and colors.

5.
Answer: option C
Explanation: ¾ of a circle in white color.

6.
Answer: option C
Explanation: 2 rectangles placed horizontally in the same size.

7.
Answer: option A
Explanation: 2 squares with a dashed outline and 1 square with a regular outline.

8.
Answer: option B
Explanation: Combos of a black arrow and a white square.

9.
Answer: option A
Explanation: Combos of 2 white triangles.

10.
Answer: option C
Explanation: Combos of 2 brackets and 2 black circles.

11.
Answer: option A
Explanation: Four-sided shapes.

12.
Answer: option B
Explanation: Two arrows pointing in the same direction.

13.
Answer: option A
Explanation: Three arrows, black, grey and white. The black arrow is always on the top.

14.
Answer: option A
Explanation: Two figures of the same type, one inside the other. The white shape is smaller.

15.
Answer: option C
Explanation: Combos of an oval shape and a black arrow.

16.
Answer: option A
Explanation: The number of lines equals the number of sides.

Paper Folding Practice Test

p.73

1.

Answer: option C

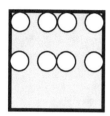

2.

Answer: option C

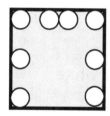

3.

Answer: option B

4.

Answer: option A

5.
Answer: option B

6.
Answer: option A

7
Answer: option A

8.
Answer: option B

9.
Answer: option A

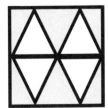

10.

Answer: option C

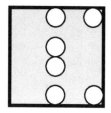

11.

Answer: option A

12.

Answer: option B

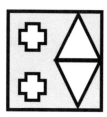

Number Puzzle Practice Test

p.81

1.
Answer: option A
Explanation: 3+1=4

2.
Answer: option A
Explanation: 6+6=12

3.
Answer: option C
Explanation: 4+6=10

4.
Answer: option A
Explanation: 6+5=11

5.
Answer: option B
Explanation: 2+5+1=8

6.
Answer: option A
Explanation: 2+3+3=8

7.
Answer: option A
Explanation: 8+4=12

8.
Answer: option C
Explanation: 1+2+1=4

9.
Answer: option C
Explanation: 4+3+3=10

10.
Answer: option A
Explanation: 4+4+4=12

11.
Answer: option B
Explanation: 1+5+1=7

12.
Answer: option B
Explanation: 2+1+3=6

Number Analogies Practice Test
p.89

1.
Answer: option A
Explanation: 1 pairs of shoes more (2 shoes more).

2.
Answer: option B
Explanation: 2 less.

3.
Answer: option A
Explanation: 5 more.

4.
Answer: option C
Explanation: 2 less.

5.
Answer: option C
Explanation: Same number of objects.

6.
Answer: option C
Explanation: 4 less.

7.
Answer: option B
Explanation: 6 more.

8.
Answer: option A
Explanation: 1 less.

9.
Answer: option B
Explanation: 7 less.

10.
Answer: option C
Explanation: 5 more.

11.
Answer: option A
Explanation: 9 less.

12.
Answer: option C
Explanation: 6 more.

13.
Answer: option A
Explanation: 2 pairs of shoes less (4 shoes less).

14.
Answer: option C
Explanation: 4 more.

15.
Answer: option B
Explanation: 2 more.

16.
Answer: option A
Explanation: 6 less.

Number Series Practice Test

p.99

1.
Answer: option C
Explanation: +1 +0, +1, +0, +1, +0, etc.
1+1=2; 2+0=2; 2+1=3; 3+0=3; 3+1=4; 4+0=4

2.
Answer: option B
Explanation: +1, +1, +0, +1, +1, +0, etc.

3.
Answer: option B
Explanation: -4,+4,-4,+4,-4,+4, etc.

4.
Answer: option B
Explanation: -3, -3, -3, +3, +3, +3, etc.

5.
Answer: option A
Explanation: -1, -1, +1, +1, -1, -1, etc.

6.
Answer: option C
Explanation: -2, +1, +1, -2, +1, +1, etc.

7.
Answer: option B
Explanation: -2, -2, -2, +2, +2, +2, etc.

8.
Answer: option A
Explanation: -3, +2, -3, +2, -3, +2, etc.

9.
Answer: option A
Explanation: +1, +2, +1, +2, +1, +2, etc.

10.
Answer: option A
Explanation: +7, -6, +1, +7, -6, +1, etc.

11.
Answer: option B
Explanation: +6, -6, +5, -5, +4, -4, etc.

12.
Answer: option C
Explanation: -3, +0, +0, -3, +0, +0, etc.

13.
Answer: option B
Explanation: -8, +8, -8, +8, -8, +8, etc.

14.
Answer: option B
Explanation: +1, +3, -1, +1, +3, -1 etc.

15.
Answer: option C
Explanation: +3, -1, +3, -1, +3, -1, etc.

16.
Answer: option B
Explanation: -3, +3, -3, +3, -3, +3 etc.

Made in United States
Troutdale, OR
01/03/2024

16644402R00073